Email Marketing Made Easy For Marketers

How to Be More Profitable on Email Marketing

By: Keith Stewart

9781634289818

PUBLISHERS NOTES

Disclaimer – Speedy Publishing LLC

This book was originally printed before 2014. This is an adapted reprint by Speedy Publishing LLC with newly updated content designed to help readers with much more accurate and timely information and data.

Speedy Publishing LLC

40 E Main Street, Newark, Delaware, 19711

Contact Us: 1-888-248-4521

Website: http://www.speedypublishing.co

REPRINTED Paperback Edition: ISBN: 9781634289818

Manufactured in the United States of America

DEDICATION

I dedicate this book to my fellow young marketers. This book is created out of will to help and inspire young professionals to earn more.

TABLE OF CONTENTS

Chapter 1- Know the Basic of Email Marketing

Email marketing is the art of making money from your email list. It is one of the ways to make money even if you don't have a fixed blog. As long as you have a list of responsive prospects of customers whom recognize you as an expert in your niche, they will definitely be up for offers of value which you provide for them.

How does this work, actually?

Well, if you have a website and you draw in some traffic, people will come, absorb some information and go away.

However, if you managed to capture their emails, you can to email them again and again – offering those nuggets of useful information or giving them offers that they might be interested in.

Marketers have recognized the potential of email marketing in generating huge profits, and have since then sought out to find the best ways to monetize their list through good email marketing practices.

This ultimate email-marketing guide aims to reveal these good practices so you can learn and apply the strategies to start raking in massive profits from your list.

Email marketing starts with your email list. What is a list?

Basically, it's short for email marketing list or email auto responder list.

The Basics

These emails are the contact information of visitors who come to your site who are looking for specific information on your niche topic.

In order to build a list, you will need to have an email auto responder set up. The two most common auto responders in the market are:

-Get response

-Aweber

It is compulsory for anyone who wishes to start an online business to get an auto responder account. This will be used to manage your subscribers and mass email your list with offers and information of interest.

Once you have an auto responder account set up, you'll have to set up a business system for collecting leads or subscribers, which I will go into detail in chapter 3 on list building essentials.

Now, with an email list, not only can you continuously build rapport with your subscribers, you can also offer them products of interest.

Traffic that comes and is not captured is a waste.

People are looking for specific information and they will leave forever once they have found out.

However, if you manage to capture their emails, you can continue to provide value and turn them into your loyal customers or followers. This is where the power of email marketing comes in.

But first, let us look at some list building essentials, for how can we make money through our list without a list to start with?

Importance of List Building

So how do you start building a list, exactly?

You will first need to set up your list funnel. It typically consists of 3 components:

1) Landing page or Squeeze Page

2) Free Gift or "Bribe"

3) Opt in box

The landing page is a simple one page website which consists of a headline, sub headline, pitch & benefits and call to action.

The headline has to be eye-catching and bolded to immediately get your reader's attention. The sub headline will reinforce the message of the headline.

The purpose of the page is to "bribe" a visitor to enter his name and email in exchange for a free gift. This could be an e-book, e-course or weekly newsletter.

The benefits are meant to explain what the reader would get from this free gift and to improve sign up rates.

Finally, in the call to action, you inform the reader that they must enter their name and email to get the free gift.

The place where the reader enters his contact information is known as the "opt in box", which can be obtained from to email auto responder host website.

Auto responders like Getresponse offer easy customizations for opt-in boxes to make boxes suit your site layout easier.

Alternatively, you can choose to put your opt in box in your blog or website to collect subscribers. The choice is entirely yours but landing pages often have higher opt in rates because visitors only have less choices – Opt in or don't as compared to blogs.

Turn Email List into a Profit

Monetization is one of the things most marketers seem to ignore until it's too late. They may throw in an affiliate link from time to time, but they ignore the big picture.

If you don't monetize your list well right from the start, you will not only be losing money, you'll be training your list to expect fewer promotions. Then, when you do start to monetize your list they may unsubscribe because of the sudden increase in promotions.

It's very important to train your list from the beginning that they are going to receive promotional messages fairly often. Don't spam them daily, but send a marketing message at least once or twice per week. This helps them remember who you are and expect those promotions.

Don't forget to send them quality content for free occasionally, as well. In fact, it's a good idea to send at least 2-3 messages with content for every 1 marketing emails you send. More people will open your messages regularly if you send them quality, informative content often, because they won't want to miss that content.

Affiliate Programs

For most people, affiliate programs will be their primary monetization method for their lists. There are two major categories of products you can promote as an affiliate – digital products and physical products.

You will soon learn which types of products your list responds best to, and you can tailor your promotions around that. For now, you might consider promoting both.

Each type has benefits and drawbacks, which we will examine. And there are thousands of different programs you could promote in each market, with millions of individual products available.

Digital Products

Information products are probably the most common type of digital product you would want to promote to your list. They can be extremely profitable in the right market.

Take, for example, the weight loss market. This is known as a "desperate market". People are desperate to lose weight, and they are willing to pay money to learn how to do so effectively.

Weight loss books, how-to videos, memberships, and meal plans make billions of dollars in revenue each year, proving that people will definitely pay for information about how to lose weight.

Digital products are available in many formats. Ebooks are the most common format, but you can also find videos, audio files, software, and other formats. Some niches respond better to different formats than others, so try promoting various types of products.

Look for products that have convincing sales letters. If the sales copy is boring, it's probably not going to convert well. You might be surprised about what people think, though. For this reason, consider testing several different products to find out which one converts best.

There are several benefits of promoting digital products. For one thing, you usually get a higher percentage of the sale price with digital products. Since they are almost pure profit and there is very little overhead, product owners can pay much more.

Additionally, digital products sometimes convert better than physical products, because the sales letters are designed to convert. Most physical products barely have two paragraphs of sales text.

Some of the most popular affiliate programs for digital products include:

• ClickBank is the most popular affiliate network for digital products. Product owners can add their products to the ClickBank network and offer affiliates a percentage of sales. ClickBank handles billing and affiliate payment, and sends product owners and affiliates payments regularly. Product owners have to go through a review process, but even so, there are thousands of products to choose from, and products are available to promote in almost any niche.

• PayDotCom is a network that is similar to ClickBank. However, instead of paying affiliates directly, they require product owners to pay affiliates. There are fewer products to choose from that ClickBank, and the quality is not always as high because there is no review process.

Physical Products

Physical products can be profitable in the right markets. In other markets, there may not be many physical products to promote, or they may not convert well. It helps to test multiple products to find out which one works best.

You don't always have to stick strictly to promoting products within your niche, either. If you had an email list targeted toward the home cooking niche, you might cross over occasionally to promote other home and garden products like herb gardening kits, kitchen equipment, and even home décor.

Physical products convert better than information in some markets. This is another reason testing is important. You may find your niche completely unresponsive to information products, but they may convert very well on physical products.

Some of the most popular affiliate programs for physical products include:

• Amazon is definitely the most popular physical product affiliate program among serious internet marketers these days. They have a massive selection of products to promote. They have books, clothes, videos, toys, jewelry, home décor, and so much more. The sales commissions are based on sales. The more you sell, the higher the percentage. But with sales commission starting at around 4%, you'll have to do a lot of volume or sell very expensive products to make good money.

• eBay's affiliate program is not as popular as it used to be, because they changed their payout system. But if you have a list built around a niche with no available products, it can be quite profitable. Just remember that you will need a very high quality website to get accepted into the program, and it can be tricky to get in.

• Commission Junction is a popular choice for people who aren't happy with Amazon's 4% commissions. Many companies pay 10% or more through Commission Junction, but they may not convert as well as the popular and generally low-priced Amazon.

Whether you promote digital or physical products, you may want to buy an additional domain to redirect your affiliate links. This will help disguise the fact that they are affiliate links, which may increase the number of people who click the links and ultimately buy.

You can use a simple redirect script, or purchase a more complex one that will track the traffic you get to your links. A good script can also help you track how effective your campaigns are.

You may want to use split-testing to find out which products convert best. This will help you find quality products you can promote to your list on a regular basis. Remember, not everyone will buy something the first time they see it, so you can promote a single product multiple times over the lifetime of your list.

There you have it; your list building system is ready. All you need is a bunch of traffic and you're all set to build a huge list!

CHAPTER 2- THE CONCEPT BEHIND EMAIL MARKETING

The most important component of an email is your headline. If your headline fails to grab your reader's attention within the first few seconds, the whole email is wasted – They won't even open it!

So what are good headlines, exactly?

It has to ignite the emotions of curiosity and don't seem like blatant pitching. You have to word it in a way that makes it seem interesting, in a way that would make someone want to open it.'

For example:

Subject: "This Hopeless Beggar Turned Into A Self Made Millionaire Within 6 Months!

A title like this creates curiosity – People would like to know how someone as disadvantaged – Like a beggar turned his life around. If even a beggar could do it, so could he/she!

Recently I came across another headline which caught my attention because it managed to include sexual vibes without coming off as spammy. Sex is a powerful emotion and strong motivator and often gets people (especially guys!) to look.

The title went something like this: "Subject: Don't let your wife know you've seen this!" As suggestive as it sounds, it worked in getting people to open it.

Try to play around with your words to find the right balance between curiosity generation and getting the message across.

Last but not least, it is highly important that your headline be relevant to the content of the email body, or else you'll be essentially training your subscribers to treat your emails like rubbish!

Copywriting

Remember, each time you email a subscriber; you take up their valuable time so your email has to either:

1) Provide really good value OR

2) Pitch something

It is highly recommended to send at least 5 emails of good value (spread out of course) before attempting to pitch something. That being said, let's look at some great copywriting tips!

The first essential thing you must know about writing good emails, is to try not to be too formal. Retain a casual tone and people will be more receptive to your emails, content and offers.

Always address your recipient, whether a simple "Hi, Hey, Hello or guess what?"

The key is to be nice in your emails but also demonstrate that you can provide immense value to your subscribers so that they will view you as an expert in your niche.

Let's talk a little about good email practices.

Email line length shouldn't be too long for better readability (preferably not more than 200 characters per line)

Always allow for "white space" between paragraphs so that everything does not look too clumped up.

Always end the note with a warm sign off or signature such as "best regards", "to your success" or "with respect" (one of my favorites).

In the end of the day, these serve as great guidelines for good copywriting but you must also try and develop your own sense of style and writing method so that your readers can identify with you.

Links

Your click-through rate would be the percentage of people who click on a link in your email from the number of people who open your emails.

In short, to get more profits, improve your clickthrough rate.

Here are some nifty tips for getting more clickthroughs:

1) Use a link cloaker. Link cloakers have the ability to mask ugly looking affiliate links and can usually customize your links to make them look more credible

(e.g. www.yoursite.com/recommends/link)

2) Shorten your URLS! Nobody likes ugly looking long links, if you must; use a URL shortener such as Tinyurl (www.tinyurl.com) or Bitly (www.bit.ly)

3) Include a call to action before the link. E.g. "Check this out now" or "Click here if you're in a hurry!" followed by the link

4) Include special bonuses as an incentive for people to click on your link. When it comes to affiliate offers, people are often looking for the most lucrative offers before they buy something.

5) Build your rapport. I cannot stress the importance of this enough. Ultimately, if you want more click-throughs, you'll have to first demonstrate value to your subscribers by giving them loads of free stuff or valuable content so that they will trust you.

In short, when you develop and practice these good email practices, your customers will become more responsive to your emails and you'll experience a "breakthrough" in your "clickthroughs".

Advanced Email Marketing Strategies

Here's how you go by creating massive profits using automated emails. In every auto responder, you can set up a series of emails which brings new subscribers through a funnel of emails over a time period.

One effective way to draw maximal conversions from your list is to first provide free valuable content before attempting to pitch. Here's an example of an effective funnel I've been using to generate passive income:

Day 1 – Introductionary email and link to free opt in gift

Day 3 – Free valuable content

Day4 – Free valuable content

Day 5 – Free valuable content

Day 6 – Give a free gift

Day 7 – Pitch offer

Day 8 – Reminder of offer

Day 10 – Follow up thank you email

I find that this often results in higher conversions. As the saying goes, you will be paid in direct proportion to the amount of value you provide to your customers.

Therefore, after receiving so much free stuff and good value from you, they are bound to purchase your product!

This is way better than just blatantly pitching them after getting their emails, which often results in opt-outs.

If you wish to take things a step further, you can offer free bonus gifts if they buy through your email link (affiliate link). When people see affiliate offers, they often look around to see which affiliate gives the most valuable gifts.

Remember, it's all about increasing click through rates and conversions, so do your best to make your subscribers like what you preach!

Errors

Here are some of the common mistakes done by marketers:

1) Blatant pitching in hope that they make a sale

-Although email marketing is a lot about numbers, blatant pitching can make even a list of thousands turn into dust as they either spam list you or become unresponsive to your offers. Which brings us to our next point.

2) Focusing too much on quantity instead of quality

-While the list in size is important, the real money is in the relationship you have with your list. So focus on making a genuine connection with your subscribers if you want to them to contribute to your coffers.

3) Using spammy looking links

-You should always invest in a link cloaker or use a free link shortener like http://bit.ly or http://tinyurl.com.

4) Using "taboo" words which increase spam score of your emails

You should avoid words that come off as spam by the spam blockers such as 'Sex', 'FREE', 'Penis', 'Viagra' or 'MLM". If you really must use these words, disrupt the spelling by putting a "." in between (e.g. make money online)

5) Finally, you should avoid using full capitals in any part of your email, whether if it's in your headline, copy or call to action. This increases spam score and sounds too salesy which lowers conversions. Treat your list with respect.

In short, good email marketing practices must be employed if you wish to build a responsive list which listen to you.

CHAPTER 3- EMAIL MARKETING AS A RECURRING INCOME

Recurring income is a blessing for any business owner, and monetizing your list with recurring income sources is always a good idea. Most niches will have products you can promote for recurring income, and in markets that don't, you could create your own.

Membership sites are an obvious choice for recurring income. Not all markets can support a membership site profitably, but in desperate niches and passionate niches, they can be major moneymakers.

If there are no viable membership sites in your niche, create your own. You'll be able to keep all of the income instead of just a portion as affiliate income, and you can promote additional products inside your membership site for more income.

It's a lot easier to create a membership site than you probably think. You can use a WordPress plugin or a simple script to manage billing and logins, and all you have to do is keep the site updated with fresh content each month.

Loss Leaders

A loss leader is a product that is sold at a loss in order to profit in another way. You could create a product of your own and sell it at a very inexpensive price in order to upsell them to another product.

For example, let's say you wanted to promote a product as an affiliate. The product costs $197, and you would get approximately $100 in commission for every sale.

You could create a similar product that was not as in-depth as the product you want to promote as an affiliate, and sell it for a very inexpensive price. Then promote the more expensive product as a kind of "upgrade" inside your product.

You could also use these inexpensive products to promote physical products. For example, you could write an information product about how to knit a sweater, and include affiliate links for knitting needles, yarn, and other knitting supplies.

Loss leaders are especially helpful for getting people used to buying from you when you're just getting started. Make sure your loss leaders are quality, so they will trust you in the future.

Your Own Products

Perhaps the most profitable thing to promote in terms of cash is your own product. Not only can you promote your product to your own list, you can also have affiliates promote your product as well.

It's a good idea to create a full range of products at various price ranges so you can reach the most customers possible. Some people may not be able to afford a $997 product, but they might be able to afford a $197 product or a $47 product. By creating a full range of offerings, you'll have something for everyone.

Here's an example of an effective product range:

• Simple eBook - $47

• Complete downloadable eBook course with 5 books - $197

• Downloadable eBook course with 5 books and 15 videos - $497

• Physical course with 5 books and 5 DVDs - $997

• One-on-one training or coaching - $1997

As you can see, the more work there is involved in creating the product and the more expense there is in creating it, the more you can charge for it.

Your least expensive product will be a very good way to introduce people to the quality of your products, so be certain you are creating extremely high-quality products even at the lower prices. The better quality your cheaper products, the more people will desire your expensive ones.

Don't forget to upsell your more expensive products in your cheaper ones. It's a missed opportunity if you fail to do this. People are never more likely to buy one of your products than they are immediately after they bought another one, especially if they're happy with your purchase.

It's very important to make sure their first experience with you is a good one, so make sure you provide top-quality support and always respond quickly to issues.

Your own products can be extremely profitable if you create a good sales funnel in order to get people to upgrade to more expensive products later. Never miss a chance to get an additional sale.

CHAPTER 4- SUBSCRIBING TO NEWSLETTERS – MARKETING STRATEGY

An e-mail newsletter is a newsletter that's delivered via e-mail that you are able to subscribe or opt-in to it.

E-mail delivery frequencies range from multiple times per day (almost never advocated) to daily to multiple times per week to weekly to bi-weekly, monthly, quarter or any periodic delivery schedule.

A few of the best newsletters are delivered daily, weekly, bi-weekly or month. Any delivery frequency longer than monthly isn't recommended.

A crucial component to a 'newsletter is the permission you give the newsletter publisher. Double or confirm-opt-in is the best technique of subscription and this implies that you not only requested to get the e-mail newsletter, but you confirmed your request to get it by clicking on a confirmation link or replying to e-mail verification. Any mailing list that doesn't call for confirmation or a subscription process is spam (unsolicited commercial e-mail).

An newsletter commonly will come in a plain ASCII text format or via a rich HTML format or allow both formats via an auto e-mail client detection technique called MIME/Multipart. You ought to never send PDF's or any other large file to your e-mail list members unless they're expecting it and can handle it getting your files.

Why do individuals publish mailing lists? It's a vital business tool to create relationships within your niche, to keep in contact with your customers or members, construct your credibility or perceived expertise in the market and drive leads, sales and/or revenue by selling products/services or advertising beside quality original content.

Among the best things you're able to do to put your e-mail marketing campaigns to work is to compose valuable content. Consider writing your content so that it does the „work" for somebody else. In any event, that work ought to relate heavily to a product or service that you supply, and act as a subtle resource for someone who might be debating on whether they should be your purchaser.

For instance, if you are a seller of particular memorabilia, write a newsletter about what qualities one ought to look for in a company selling memorabilia.

A lot of individuals might be concerned that they may be getting ripped-off by somebody selling fake memorabilia, so make them comfortable purchasing from you by highlighting what makes you legitimate... in a neutral way. Speak about certifications and associations that the true sellers have and belong to.

Discuss the nitty-gritty details of how crucial a high-res photograph is in confirming the validity of an item. Supply valuable resources that back your claim, and make your newsletter reach out to provide them advice.

By utilizing this sort of technique, you are able to easily highlight those strengths that your company has while providing a really enlightening newsletter for your subscribers. This produces a valuable resource that they would want to pass on to their acquaintances and co-workers all the while having your brand attached.

Although newsletters may be an excellent way to feature a new product or service that you provide, you have to think about what makes it worth reading, and more significantly, how can it make you stick out as an expert!

Why You Should

Previously in my career, I naively sent traffic straight to merchant web sites utilizing affiliate links. Sometime later, I produced landing pages so visitors would "see" something new before making it to the merchant web site, while I neglected to utilize an opt in form.

Half-baked, yep... I was a newcomer. I rapidly discovered centering on driving traffic for one-time sales was only profiting the merchant, not me.

That's when I recognized the importance of follow through. Although my old landing pages were filled up with targeted material and personalized data, sales become more consistent till adding an auto responder opt in form... granting me the lucrative chance to follow through with visitors.

This leads to the number 1 reason to utilize e-mail marketing to make revenue on the net...

Following through provides you the chance to expose your product or offer to visitors beyond their initial visit. It likewise provides you the opportunity to present your offer in more detail and answer general questions (FAQs) before they're even inquired.

Supplying answers in your follow through e-mails before they're asked (reading the subscriber's mind) may slide sales right to you.

What's excellent is when visitors opt into your form to get additional info; they're expressing an interest to learn more & allowing you permission to contact them once again. It puts you in a great selling position. You're now presented another prime chance to "catch the sale".

How great is that? Right! Simply remember...

- E-mail Marketing = More Exposure = More chances To follow through
- With prime Content = More revenue & Sales
- Which feeds nicely into the 2nd rationality...

Hold on! Before you progress, print this. I guarantee you that you'll get much more benefit from studying the data, instead of merely browsing through it on your computer. Before you even start reading... print out on paper. Get an ink pen. Circle or emphasize items of importance to you.

Doodle ideas and notes in the margins. Write up action steps.

Rationality No. 2 - one e-mail may equal mass gross sales. Once you've affected a trustworthy relationship with subscribers by sharing select free content and making recommendations that actively helps them in some manner, you'll have cultivated a list where one e-mail promotion may equal monumental sales. A privilege kin to having an ATM in your desktop.

There's nothing more stimulating than making an excellent product recommendation to your e-mail list and having them react with enthusiastic sales that roll in almost instantly. Just be careful to never take your list for granted; they're real-live individuals. Treat them with honor, not cash machines.

The great thing about an automated marketing system that systematically pulls profits is that it's the closest thing to being able to "set & forget it".

E-mail marketing automation decidedly beats offline methods of follow through any day.

Would you rather spend a long time pitching prospects, answering questions, arming yourself with rebuttals, handling with rejection... all aimed to capture one sale -or- load an auto responder with substantive material equally monetized with fruitful offers, set to act as your automated sales department?

I'd follow the latter, I'm sure you concur. That is, if you're serious about having a successful net business that systematically makes you revenue & you comprehend the value of time/freedom.

Automation is key to successful development and profitability, in both the short and long-term. Having an automated e-mail scheme for interested leads to opt into directly puts you in position to get automated sales. Automation lets you leverage sales in innumerable, creative ways.

Millionaires comprehend the might of automation & leverage: So if you ever doubt whether e-mail marketing is worth establishing as a central function of your marketing technique, remind yourself:

1) Multiple follow through chances to get sales,

2) One e-mail may = large-scale sales,

3) Leveraged automation.

CHAPTER 5- HOW TO PROPERLY SEND OUT NEWSLETTER

Several believe single opt in is better, in that they opt not to send a visitor through too many channels in order to get information...trusting less channels, more sales.

This might be true, dependent on the offer and the list, however with single opt in normally comes more SPAM complaints for an assortment of reasons:

• Don't care for the offer...

• Mad because you're promoting something for cash, even if you're likewise supplying free helpful data...

• Sending out a follow-up e-mail 2 days or 2 weeks later

It may be anything. The thing is when these complaints mount, you have no recourse to prove these were legitimate requests made through your opt in form. And if they don't holler spam, single opt in tends to clog your list with non-responsive, tire-kickers. Common reason being, opt in's are not made to affirm "Yes, I require this info."

Once opt in's take the time to go into their inbox & click a "confirmation link", they're re-affirming, "Yes, I decidedly wish to get this info."

When you require a potential subscriber carry out the motions of confirming, you're pulling them out of simply acting passively, out of instinct.

You're making them not only state, "yep." (passively, unconsciously) but "Yes, Yes!". Just in case you haven't figured it out by now, I favor double opt in.

Mainly as I spend time and effort producing quality material for my subscribers and I wish those who request it to truly want it, pay attention when they get it and really value what I'm providing.

Reasons For Double Opt In

1 - You wish visitors who subscribe to pay attention to what you're providing - double opt in does just that. Sorry people but human nature doesn't by nature (or on first impulse) value opportunities or info that's readily given to them. Pitiful but true. It's up to you make subscribers realize the info they're requesting as being useful and highly-important.

2 - you've confirmed data (proof) that somebody at that e-mail address utilized that name on that date at that time to request info

be sent after visiting your site and they really clicked a link to confirm that the request was made.

Even though anybody may cry foul, or in that instance SPAM, you're safe, protected... as you now have valid proof on your side. This is how come explaining to visitors "How To Confirm" and "How To Unsubscribe" helps to diminish spam complaints.

You want it clear-cut that if they no longer wish to get info from you, then they may simply click unsubscribe in the email.

3 - You cultivate & sustain a clean, responsive e-mail list. E-mail marketing is the simplest way to make fast, consistent long-term revenue and how you do it's crucial in cultivating a highly-responsive list. A highly-responsive list comes as a consequence of earned trust and respect.

You likewise earn a particular amount of respect when somebody has to confirm their request, whether it's apparent or not. Because what you're stating is, "If you wish this material, you'll do what I'm asking you to do to acquire it."

True subscribers will abide by your request as the initial impression is...

1) You recognize what you're doing and

2) You're in it for the long run

You're likewise stating you respect them reciprocally. As a pro, you're taking extra measures to ensure their data is going to the right place. Individuals respect professionalism.

Individuals likewise value what is made to appear valuable. The value is evident once they get the info and it turns out to be truly excellent content that does something for them. If you're provided content lives up to its sensed value, you've gained a subscriber's trust.

Maintain your newly built reputation and subscribers will trust, worth & respect what you have to state.

There are debates for single opt in option, however my experience has found them to be really weak and not worth their weight. I detest SPAM as much as the next individual and as an e-mail marketer, I certainly don't want "spam charges" cluttering my business inbox. If a spam

Charge does arise; I may readily annihilate it with valid proof.

Separate "the genuine & serious" from "unconscious lookie-loos & freebie-seekers" as much as conceivable. Utilizing double opt in as part of your e-mail marketing technique lets you do just that. The gains are decidedly worth the effort.

CHAPTER 6- MORE TIPS ON HOW TO INCREASE YOUR REVENUE

Among the most crucial assets to making revenue online is having your own opt in list.

To be more particular, a motivated opt in list that's responsive to your material.

If you've been marketing online for an adequate amount of time, you comprehend the truth behind... the revenue is in the list.

This stems from the truth that the sum of money you make online is instantly related to the size of your e-mail marketing list.

1.

Hold in mind it's not all quantity, quality is predominant. You wish to systematically offer your list great happy they may utilize because when you do, you deliver to an ultra-responsive e-mail list that will reward you with sustainable profits. Anybody may have a list that reaches well into the 1000s, but if its dead- it's purposeless. A full of life, responsive list, even if it's only amounts to a couple 100 subscribers, is gold.

Now that I've founded the importance of having an opt in list, here are ways to hike your opt in rates and produce a strong, responsive

"Sell" your offer to acquire potential subscribers. You have to provide visitors a compelling reason to opt into your list. The most beneficial ways to sell an offer, especially ones that are free, are to...

1. Supply a free report answering an urgent question your niche is facing or providing a result-driven solution.

2. List leastways 3 bulleted reasons of what your offer may do for them. Answer - "what's in it for me"? Bullet points are "scannable"; they provide

Instantaneous data at a glance and are proven to better opt in rates.

3. Describe to a potential subscriber how they'll benefit from being on your specific list.

4. Produce a highly-informative Ecorse. E-mail mini-courses packed with useful content are great opt in motivators. 3, 5 or 7 days are fruitful length numbers, spread a day or two apart. Your Ecorse title may be as simple as "5 Ways To Double Profits. Whatever it is, you need to make it compelling, results-driven and related to your niche.

5. Along with supplying excellent material, let your personality shine through to make your Ecorse authentic and relatable.

3. Set your first installment to be handed over at once. You need to "satisfy" your opt in straight off while your offer is still fresh in their minds.

A different marvelous way to boost opt in rates is to offer a useful eBook, audio or video tutorial.

6. Useful in being a product that you are able to actually sell and make income from... only in this case you're offering this excellent data free only to subscribers of your e-zine or newsletter.

7. Attach a truthful value number to it. If your offer lives up to its worth in happy, you'll earn the trust of your subscriber and they'll be far less likely to unsubscribe or opt out after getting your info.

8. The basic purpose of your opt in (landing or squeeze) page ought to be to capture as many legitimate names and e-mail addresses as possible. Make this your #1 resolution.

9. Only provide visitor 2 choices, opt in or leave. Avoid placing any outbound links on your opt in page - links that will lead anyplace other than to submit a name and e-mail address. Ignoring this tip may severely dilute opt in results and will be counter-productive to

your traffic generation attempts. So remember, allow 2 options solely.

Following these proven opt in e-mail marketing tips won't only significantly boost opt in rates but turn your e-mail list into an ultra responsive, lucrative resource.

Some Tips

The nice thing about e-mail marketing is it allows you to leverage your efforts twenty-four/seven utilizing automation. Following through with visitors beyond their initial visit provides multiplied chances for exposure (exposing your site/offer over and over).

To be more particular... offering something useful via an opt in form on your site, confirming their request for info and supplying relevant, valuable email follow-up.

Here are the best e-mail marketing tips to systematically follow for success:

1 - Provide a free report or gift (software download/app) thru an opt in form in exchange for visitor's name and e-mail address. Providing free info is a great way to build a list fast. Remember; make the free offer unparalleled & prosperous to access.

2 - Confirm the opt in request to prevent spam complaints. Bearing a record of the date, time, name and e-mail utilized in making the request protects you. It shows you take your business relationship earnestly and helps keep your e-mail list "clean" as it grows.

3 - Flip-flop relevant, high-quality happy with useful offers. This ought to be info that meets the particular needs of your list. For this specific tip, here are a few helpful steps to abide by...

- Send helpful info & "how to" tips that are relevant and straight to the point

- Keep e-mails short and easy-to-read

- Forever proof-read and make the essential corrections

- Call for not more than 1 action per e-mail... meaning whatever action you want; have it lead to one result... i.e. if you supply 2 links in an e-mail, have them go to 1 place (to a site or to a download page). Asking subscribers to do more than 1 affair causes in-action or "choice paralysis".

- Put your hyperlink at the beginning & end of every e-mail - both leading to the same place.

CHAPTER 7- USEFUL TRUTHS ABOUT EMAIL

Even though this course is on email marketing, you need to come to terms with some truths about it. For one, email marketing is not as effective as it used to be. To be more exact, email marketing started to lose the effectiveness it used to have prior to Facebook's popularity.

As of this time of writing, more Internet users spend more time checking their Facebook and Twitter account daily. Slightly more than half of the global Internet users have a Facebook account and people aged 20 and below prefer to check their Facebook account for messages than their email! You can say the same for Twitter in spite of its 140 character limitations per direct messaging.

And get this: GMail, one of the leading email providers, had recently implemented the 'priority markers' feature allowing their users to mark selected emails as important and thus change the ways people prioritize their emails for reading consumption every time they check their Inbox. And let's be honest: promotional emails rarely ever reach PRIORITY status!

Then they a smart system that detects and filters spam emails and it gets tweaked frequently, therefore making even legit email marketing harder.

Given those reasons, am I implying that email marketing is dying? In spite of these factors, email marketing is still far from dying because it remains an essential Internet feature!

But I want to bring those truths to your attention because you need to understand that there will always be new technology, and technology changes things.

Plus don't forget the sheer volume of spams, ads, and other marketers also using email are competing for your prospect's attention just like you.

This means you need to employ different, more effective tactics to capture your prospect's attention and get him to act on YOUR email instead of your competitors!

This is imperative especially if you happen to operate in a niche that is highly competitive, and that it is not uncommon for people to subscribe to more than one mailing lists – examples like, but not limited to: Internet Marketing, business opportunities, Multi-Level Marketing, Forex, real estate, weight loss, dating and relationship.

In other words, for almost every subscriber who joins your mailing list you can safely assume that they are also on your competitors mailing lists. And you know how buyers can be harsh and unforgiving when it comes to comparison shopping!

Speaking of shopping, I want to get this huge popular misconception out of the way about 'giving away free content'. Here are three main reasons why giving away free content to your subscribers is pure nonsense:

• First of all, it defeats your true purpose and goal of building a mailing list. The reason you build a list is to convert your prospects into buyers, and buyers into long time customers! This is essentially why you are building a list ripe to email market and do it for profits!

• Secondly, when you send a 'content only' email your subscribers don't take action. I guarantee you that. Send them an email containing a 400 word article on tips and how to do something – with no links or call to action whatsoever – and you will never make a red cent. And worse, your subscribers are usually busy people they rarely have time to read a lengthy 'content' email!

• Most amateur email marketers reason that giving content is important because it will reduce their un-subscription rates while making their subscribers happy. This is B.S. again on two other counts. One, you can never please everyone. Two, when people realize they don't have time to read or 'consume' your emails they will hit the un-subscribe link at the bottom of the email, thus you still get un-subscriptions!

Don't just take my word for it. Take a look at what leading Internet companies are doing in the area of email marketing.

If you are on Amazon's mailing list or bought something from them before, notice that Amazon.com always sends promotional email offers recommending other products related to your previous purchase? They do not give free tips. They do not give 'how tos' and they certainly don't give free content. They are in business of selling you more stuff, and that's coming from an Internet company that 34 billion dollars a year in revenue!

Groupon.com always send bulks of discount offers in their emails. But they never give free content. It's always been promotional emails all the way!

These are just prime examples. Subscribe to the list of any big companies and you will see they always send out email offers; not free content!

That said, forget about trying to please everyone with 'free content' – the true purpose of email marketing is to simply convert as many prospects into buyers as possible. Period.

And if you already have a list of buyers, your next goal is to get them to become lifetime customers, like what Amazon.com and Groupon.com are doing!

Because contrary to the popular opinion you always hear on marketing forums (shame on them actually) and what a handful of your subscribers think you should be providing... it's NEVER about giving away free content!

But does that mean you should go all sales pitchy? Here's the catch: ironically, you also cannot approach your subscribers with a 'hard sell' tone! (There's a reason why spam filters were created, and what un-subscribe links are for!)

If 'in your face' selling worked effectively, everyone would be resorting to spam methods. And even if you had gotten your subscriber's permission to email them (hence opt-in), this does not give you the incentive to send 'hard sell' emails to them.

This is the frustrating part a lot of email marketers are facing with immense confusion. On one side, you have amateur email marketers who think that giving away free content will build their credibility and trust (not really true). On the other side, you have annoying email marketers who try to hard sell in their emails, they are actually no different from spammers even with the benefit of their subscribers permission to email them!

So what's the solution? You don't sell in the email; you merely pre-sell! I will be covering more on this in the later section of the course.

When it comes to boosting your email open rates, you are competing for the attention of your readers. And even if the competition was minor, you still need to give the reader a compelling reason to open your email instead of deleting it with the rest of the unimportant emails.

Email marketing, like everything else, is a numbers game. And there are ways to increase your email open rates. It can never be 100% - even personal emails get lost or deleted by mistake, and all the more with commercial emails. So the only variable you are in control is to boost your email open rates so as many subscribers in your list opens it as possible.

Let's start with the email subject line since it's the 'make or break' impression. The rule of thumb is to keep the length of the subject line anywhere in between 25 and 45 characters long. Anything longer than 50 characters and you might experience a drop in your open rates! Because people use different email clients or programs, and depending on what they are using they can read only so many characters per line. Thus the safest thing to do is keep it under 45 characters.

Another open rate killer is CAPITALIZING ALL YOUR LETTERS. Online, it comes across as if it's shouting and therefore it's treated as rude and obnoxious. Second, it's harder to read. For example, compare these two email subject lines:

WHY I LOVE MINI LAUNCHES...

and

Why I love mini launches...

Note that the capitalized subject line is harder to read than the other.

Another danger is overusing the word "FREE". Modern spam filters recognize FREE as one of the many common spam words and it's easy to rake up negative scores that might result in your email getting filtered to spam or bulk folders. Even if not for that reason, you will foster a 'freebie seeker' relationship with your subscribers which is another problem you don't want to have as a marketer.

So in the event you're giving something away for free, I recommend using other synonyms like: zero cost, no cost, on the house, and no strings attached.

SENDER NAME. Keep it below 20 to 25 characters. Also, don't add special characters like *** to your sender name because contrary to what you may think, doing this actually kills your open rates too! You might think you would have stood out from the rest of the email senders but in actual fact, this is almost

associated with other spammer activity that use special characters in their sender name. So keep it simple, just use your name as it is. And if the email is sent from a company, your company name should be in 1 to 2 words (preferably just one, like "Amazon" and "Groupon").

When sending out the next email, make it a habit to put in some figures. Example: "Your $100K a year blueprint video". You don't have to add figures in every single email subject line you put out but it is preferable that you make it a common practice. Other examples include:

• 7 reasons why I love mini launches...

• Why it took 3 desperate man to kidnap a guru...

• How 3 words can get you any women you want...

Also note that I fix a "..." that leaves the sentence incomplete. From my testing experience, I learned that emails that end with "..." produce higher open rates than those without! You can say this is like a 'cliff hanger' feature and if it builds enough curiosity your reader will open the email to follow through the story.

I also found that the word BONUS gives a +17% open rate increase! This is another reason why I don't like to use the word FREE. Example: "Inspiration DNA Videos + $1997 Mega Bonus"

Implying a scarcity factor produced an extra +12% increase in my open rates compared to when I did not mention it at all in my subject line. Example: [20 left] Private Label Rights to 3 Bestselling Software...

However don't overuse crazy characters. My definition of 'crazy characters' are anything like this:

■ ■ ■ How to pick any profitable stock with 7 secret methods ■ ■ ■

If you haven't noticed, a lot of spam emails usually include crazy characters that cannot be read or interpreted. If you also over use characters like! + - % it can also kill your email open rates. In your effort of trying to get attention, it will not only destroy your credibility you will get a lot of un-subscribes too!

Also, don't write your subject lines in an attempt to fool the spam filters by plotting a full stop in between the 'spam worthy' words like:

Here is your f.ree gift

$2,OOO a month gua.ran.teed

This makes your email appear less professional. While it was acceptable practice a few years ago, I discovered this practice is considered phased out by today's email marketing standards.

CHAPTER 8- WHAT IS THE PERFECT TIME TO SEND EMAIL?

The email subject line being one variable factor, the other is timing. The often asked question is, "when is the best time in the day to send out an email?" While you cannot configure that with sequential auto responders, you are in control as to when you want to send out time sensitive email blast to your mailing list.

I share this conclusion with other email marketers who had tested and tracked their responses; sending your email between 7:00 AM and 9:00 AM Eastern Time produces the highest open rates than any other given time. This is true if your subscribers are based mostly in North America or international. While Americans in general check their email before leaving the house for work (or start their day off in that fashion before work), Asians who live 9 to 12 hours ahead of Eastern Time have the opposite habit: they prefer to relax and check their emails after work.

That said, this is not really a surprise why many product launches prefer to launch at this time. However it's also interesting to note that responses start to drop after 10:00 AM – that's how much difference emailing one hour later can make! And if you mail out any time after 1:00 PM (which is past midnight for the other side of the world), you can lose 35% of the responses!

By 3:00 PM Eastern Time you can lose about half or more of your responses than if you had mailed out earlier in the morning. So if you are late for sending out a promotion email, it is advised that you postpone the email promotion to the following day, and email out promptly at 7:00 to 9:00 AM Eastern Time or risk getting bad email open rates and responses. And if you are doing a product launch, it is advisable to start it in the morning rather than in the afternoon Eastern Time.

What about the best days to send? From my mailings, I found that Tuesdays and Fridays produce the highest email open rates. While Tuesdays is probably not a surprise (since a lot of product launches favor Tuesdays), Fridays produce high email open rates as it's almost the weekend and people in general are more relaxed after working the week. Again, this is true for mailing in the Internet Marketing niche as far as that is concerned.

Mondays and Thursdays bring average email open rates, which are still okay. In fact for some email marketers, they prefer not to mail out on Mondays because of the "Monday Blues" the general masses is having.

Wednesdays, in my finding, produce the lowest response of all weekdays.

What about Saturdays and Sundays? After one full year of testing the weekend, I have concluded that weekends bring the worst response of all days! It is as low as less than half of the average responses on weekdays even!

So depending on your email frequency, it is best to pick strictly weekdays and try to avoid Wednesdays where possible. As far as weekends are concerned, you're probably better off being away from the computer as most people are during that time or work on something else.

Even if you want to drop an email to your subscribers, this is the best time to get your subscribers to do some fun things like quizzes, surveys, read your latest blog post, and so on.

Email Body

You should keep your email body anywhere between 150 to 300 words maximum. Ideally, around 200 words is good. I keep all my emails in word format so I can see my word count in a glance. Even though you can virtually write nearly an infinite amount of words in an email, the average Internet user's attention span is really short. Juggling between being busy, surfing on impulse and other things begging for his attention, you have only a couple of minutes (or even less than that!) to say what you want to say.

Also format your email to 55 characters per line. I use this free tool called NoteTab – you can download the freeware at http://notetab.com/ I use this to format my emails automatically and wrap them to 55 characters per line.

As established earlier, different users use different email clients. For some, their email client recognizes up to 55-65 characters per line. And then there are those that read all the way from one end of the screen to the other! This makes it difficult for people to read especially if they are using a wide LCD screen. To aid in easy reading, break into paragraphs of 1 to 3 lines.

With huge blobs of text, this email is harder to read. But when you format it into 55 characters per line and break into easy-to-read paragraphs each containing no more than 1 to 3 lines, this becomes easier to digest and comfortable for the eyes.

Call to Action

Essentially, the goal of your email is to get your subscriber to click on the link to follow through your promotion email and go to the sales letter or site of offer. The Call To Action doesn't have to be complicated; you merely need to draw attention to the link.

• Here Is Your Special Discount Link:

• Click Here Now For More Info:

• Reserve Your Spot Now:

• Get All The Juicy Details Here:

It's not groundbreaking but I found that putting the call to action line in uppercase for each starting word actually increases the click through by 6% to 7% more!

To maximize the call to action (the click through rate for your links in your email) you should repeat the link 3 times throughout the email body in any of the following fashion:

• BEGINNING, END and P.S.

Or

• BEGINNING, MIDDLE and END (if no P.S.)

Do not include more than 3 URLs because some spam filters perceive emails with more than 3 links to be of spam material. Thus if you add more than 3 URLs you are flirting with getting your emails filtered. This is why you shouldn't attempt to stuff too many things, or more than one main message, into a single email. Dedicate one email to one main message. And that all 3 URLs go to the same link.

However, you should avoid using free link redirect services like TinyURL and Bit.ly for your email marketing – they are actually CTR killers from my testing and my business friends who do email marketing too!

(As of now, emails including bit.ly links risk getting into spam folders for GMail and Hotmail users. Whether this will be rectified or not remains to be seen.)

Also, you won't be able to track your click throughs from most of these free redirect services (except maybe if you upgraded your account). Nothing beats having your own domain and link redirect.

SUMMARY

Probably the most important message of this email marketing guide is that you should respect your list like how you would like to be respected and also learn and apply good email marketing practices.

As much as you'd like to see commissions pouring in from one email, the proper groundwork and relationship, building has to be done if you want to have a responsive list.

A good way to learn additional marketing techniques that work is to model the emails of successful marketers and copy their styles, techniques and tone to suit your personal style.

It's crucial to stress that anybody considering e-mail marketing must read up on the subject of permission and spam. If you don't comprehend the importance of permission and the risks of ignoring it, then you may be heading for commercial disaster.

Don't panic, though. It's in reality relatively easy to ensure that the address lists you use or build yourself are permission-based.

Also, don't forget to track click-throughs and open rates of your emails to see what type of copywriting styles work best for your list.

I wish you all the best in your email marketing efforts!

Warm Regards

About The Author

Keith Stewart has a wide range of experience and knowledge in marketing, because of this many firms and institutions believe in his abilities and skills. Keith works hand in hand with consultants, marketing professionals, coaches and other financial professionals to help in marketing strategy and to create more attractive ads.

Same dedication and effort that Keith poured in email marketing. He found out a better opportunity online. He wants to show to entrepreneurs, marketers, consultants and other financial professionals that there is money in email marketing.

www.ingramcontent.com/pod-product-compliance
Lightning Source LLC
Chambersburg PA
CBHW070901070326
40690CB00009B/1937